IS THE ROOM

poems

Rosetta Ballew-Jennings

IS THE ROOM

poems

Rosetta Ballew-Jennings

cover art by Grace Roselli

Jaded Ibis Press
sustainable literature by digital means™
an imprint of Jaded Ibis Productions U.S.A.

ISBN: 978-1-937543-40-2

Library of Congress Control Number: 2013911189

Printed in the United States of America. No part of this book may
be used or reproduced in any manner whatsoever without written
permission from the publisher, except in the case of brief quotations
embodied in critical articles and reviews. For information please email:
questions@jadedibisproductions.com

Published by Jaded Ibis Press, *sustainable literature by digital means*™ An
imprint of Jaded Ibis Productions, LLC, Seattle, WA USA

Cover by Grace Roselli.

This book is available in multiple editions and formats. Visit our website
for more information: jadedibisproductions.com

For Glenn Eugene and Diana Rose,
who read to me first

AKNOWLEDGEMENTS

My appreciation to the journals in which these poems
first appeared:

The Laurel Review
"Waiting on the noon parade," "Miscellaneous locations," and "As
if she were something opened,"

Anti-
"The sky is waiting" and "The construction site"

My gratitude, as well, to the fierce and lovely Kathleen Peirce – to
the depth of her, her pies, and her velvet couch.

To John Gallaher, who first handed me Jean Valentine, among
other things, thank you, friend.

And, to the rarely silent A.J. Ortega, thanks, always, for your ears.

Additional thanks to Jaded Ibis Press, Debra Di Blasi, and Sam
Witt for the needed, conscious, risk-taking work you do every day
and for the support and enthusiasm that led to this publication.

Finally, to Alec, my love.

CONTENTS

[...]

What draws you on so hard?
        You would like to think
about resting
a minute on the mobbed walk or
the electrocardiograph table
to ask about the house there—dark ,
stone, floating over the edge of the buildings,
        someone, something, it may be, inside—
but you can't stop here: the dangerous air,
the crowds, the lights, the hardening Indian Summer. . .

        strange quiet,
[...]

                                        – Jean Valentine
                                from "Autumn Day"

To all:

A woman called
saying she was to call our number.

She did not know who she was calling for. Or
could not remember   or
could not say   so

if you called a woman
who was to call you

she did.

Because places dissolve

I will say goodbye.
as, I might not see you later, or tomorrow, or noon
or ever   beyond this
I do not know.
Focused on my blue shoes, I may step in front of a green bus and
then
I may not see you again or
as you are, but instead
maybe I will see you as a donkey and me as a cat
and maybe we will not meet at noon, but at dusk
and then I may know you by the same name, or not
a sound, then, up close, or not.
Maybe the distance, then, will be you
and I could be the sound or the sound you think you heard
and we will only know each other by the vibrations of the earth.

Hallway landscape

Behind the doors are the halls.

We know this and we believe it. Behind the doors, the open
throats
to the outside, to the twelve green carts
abandoned and, we say, distraught,
frozen mid-roam
to the woman reading the mail with her feet in the leaves
and the dirt
under and around the picnic table.

The structure and the opening.

And between the doors and the hallways,
between the here and there,
are mailboxes. One hundred forty four boxes, names reversed
and lined
in a way we've never seen ourselves,
or so we say

Absorbed
and then set gentle—

toe and then heel in the hall.

What he saw

He saw that she liked oranges red sweaters babies' toes and he saw that she walked with her right knee pointed in and her lips fissured again and again when other people were talking and she was thinking about gardening or wedding cakes he saw that she liked to smell good with earthy smells and not French ones and not Italian ones and Spanish ones she sometimes liked if they were bought for a special occasion and in a pretty bottle. He saw that she collected pretty bottles with and without stoppers he saw that sometimes when she was excited and talking to him he needed to remind her to stop at the single stop light on the corner on way to the grocery store he saw when they were there her eyes were held by a bucket of sugar on the lower shelf he saw that they never needed that much sugar that she wanted it and that she wanted people to use that much sugar and he saw that she wanted people he saw that she was playful after dinner and was teased when he acted irritated by it and became more playful he saw that she tickled and pinched and he saw that she bit and he saw that he could carry her outside without protest and put her in the cabin of the old wooden houseboat he saw that she swept it sometimes and he saw her under him under the small cabin window he saw that the window was like the kind that are on the sides of toy ships or for unwieldy pirates in coloring books he saw that she would probably act like one of those pirates later and put her head through the window he saw that now they were having sex saw that the spiders in the corners watched he saw red curls he saw always he saw if they got too close he saw her under him he saw that she liked oranges red sweaters babies' toes he saw that she walked with her right knee pointed in.

House

1.

The blue bowl is down

The woman in your dreams is the woman
is the woman in your dreams

The writing of the old letters is soft and slipping
and we are dangerous

Don't separate blue and bowl and
down

The house is around you
and the house can do only
what a house can do

2.

The house is coming down

Or maybe it is rattling,
slipping back into itself

The ground and the grass are there
They are applauding your measures

And Fiona loves the night
with the Appalachian rhyme
loves it red, loves it blue, loves it orange

You won't like the spaces here
something about the disconnect

It is a whisper and it is saying
you may not be
the you of here

3.

We go looking room to room turning on the lights
turning off the lights, saying our names aloud

The bowls are upside down
A line of islands or prisons
depending on which curve you see

You are noting this to tell the woman
know that you might tell her
about your knee
jewel beetles
the nature of hinges instead

A bowl is blue
filled with water

We call it moon on the landscape
of the walnut floor

4.

You may not be you
So we decide to mostly sit and name one another
Seven months

And by now the others are noticing
They see the names

My eyelashes and your hands

And we hear from across the room that the doors
have been calling us

We send the bowls, the blue ones   We'll go later

5.

The rug is collecting the lights of the room
and now it is a door

Fall through it

Show your eyes

Dance shirtless

The window next to the corner
of the rug has twelve panes
of glass that dismantle seven shadows

The house is growing dark

Lay in it
and see how your lips change

6.

With her hands nearly clasped

She called for the rooms

You and the halls came

The windows and invited crickets
waited (closely) for her to

close her eyes

and call once more

The rest of us go about
turning on lamps

7.

The hills are hills, matted and brown until
they are the humps of camels, brown and matted

We can see them change back and forth Though,
it takes time for Fiona to find the rhythm
so that what she sees
is not part hill and part camel

This is fine
And as we look for rapid eye movement
Eye hill camel hill eye camel hill eye

We are fine being outside the scene
until I consider the problem of closets

8.

The diameter of the woman
is more than we
expected

It keeps us up at nights,
leads us down highways at dark, takes us up
the blue hallway where we phone friends
come from pines and rivers

And in the blue hallway is the woman
face after face after

Three are asking for flowers
One for sound cursive R's,
a beautiful S   The next,
a breath from a cedar wardrobe

9.

We are always arriving or leaving
Arrived   Left
A point in motion is a line
Or points in line are motion

The doors, all open, become the hallways
The door becomes invisible

A thing is left that we call door so that there is an inside
Lots of people like that
And the two-year olds and the four-year olds
start using the same wave, the same voices
on both sides of the doors

We have left

The light is green and we are looking for doorknobs
In a moment we'll wave from the distance

You'll ask Fiona about the color of my scarf, expecting it
to come closer
In wait, you will speak of ladybug legs in the screens of
the doors, table legs—

of things that can be said

Your mail,
and the package from Sunday, is in the vestibule

The sky is waiting

To know where you are

What is too much to say.

I see you?
I see you on the sidewalk.   I see
you in your tee shirt.   I see you in the water.
I see the rebar in the concrete through your ribs
I do not see you separate.

What is too much to say What is too much to say

To save you. To save me from_____.
To   .

They are saying your name collectively.
The voices left open to the lit and unlit sky.

Rosetta Ballew-Jennings

A moonbird, unfeathered

For Jennie

The curve of a fish belly and back
two lips and eyes
the non-existent ears
are what you need

to live.

It is no secret. You are known for it.
The curves of natures held tight to your belly button—
only the grass could explain it more fully.

We want to be happy so we laugh
draw circles and ducks and beavers together.
Owls on our backs.

We overlook the impossible

blue and green river from precarious positions.

You are hanging there.

Very soft and not noticeable

And all the people ran away,
the women holding bunches of lilacs,
the men holding the women.

And in the back
a woman wept, smiling,
and would cry herself to sleep
through bunches of lilacs,
and men, where there is only a flame.

I've stood at my window all day.
All day, the corners of the window.
The paint on the wall.

And I have always been lonely
among mothers
and other strangers.

Rosetta Ballew-Jennings

Sleeping alone on the South Fork river

There are children
small and dainty with pretty pink feet
that run through the cornfields
brown eyes peering through the stalks
They eat in the greasy oaks
high above the ground
                              and the squirrels
but I find them asleep
on the South Fork River, lying head to toe,
eyelashes tangled in the mossy banks
fingers floating in the water
I am lonely for them
and wade through the water
I complicate my fingers in their curly hair
and breathe their music
through mud-streaked bellybuttons

The contrast of these mornings

To curl, to fondle. The way we move.

To remove or pervert.
To go away, to shake relief.

I have friends not so very far away.

You know,
I have friends in Paris.

A day breaking and cold breeze,
the constant headaches.

Any set of items lined up in space,
something without a middle.

Any way I might turn from the dresser.
Something I cannot find.

Lying in bed

Lying in bed I said something about cereal
and forgetting the milk.
Shaved light and kisses.
I don't love you,
or something like that.

There's a field I used to go lie in
as a girl. Two trees. And the sun
through those trees across
the tall grass, and the shadow
of the trees.

Time is strange, fractured space
that feels something like truth
or the implication of it.

General semantics

I am needing to speak to you

behind this door

with no handle.

Rosetta Ballew-Jennings

Impending nuptial dreams

Everything is wrapped
in gold and white
light and cloth.

Then.   Fire.

Even the bride is a streak
          of wild light.

Orange and red blindness

every night.

To keep the house from burning down

You had the good sense
not to sleep at night

to keep the house from burning down.

You.

The baby sister wailing
                    sleeping
                    playing
                    insane
The brother waiting
at the still small tree
in the front yard
where everyone had agreed to meet.

Instead, you made friends with a man
who was only a shadow.
A criminal who lived in the woods
and sat on the air conditioner outside
the bedroom window
to tell you about his day
to listen about yours.

He lived on the outside of the purple curtains
and you loved him like a woman
in your noon dreams with the house
burning down around you both.
delighted.

Mother in the kitchen with sandwiches.

Rosetta Ballew-Jennings

This thing I have found
when you are sleepy and
drunk and still not wanting
of fireplaces and candles.

The sidewalk collects a pretty girl

April or May, and sun through leaves. Sometimes
being still is not being dead or being
asleep, but sustained.

The half full cup
of the stagnant pond. The boy
plagues the window, watching
the girl

lying quiet and still on the sidewalk
face upward and closed, and her
palms settled on pocked concrete.

Waiting for her
He tells me
"[   ]to move or to move something
just by being there like that."
He tells me.

The moment is going nowhere.

I object to something in the background motion
of the house, and then,

want for sudden rain.

Today I saw a woman climb a tree and weep

The hum of the new air conditioner
and the scratching of furniture and boxes.

Today we moved my brother into his first house.

Small, hot, and crowded.
The bustling sweat of a summer move. A good move.

It was somewhere near 1:30 in the morning.
I watched her
from the basement stairs.

I saw a woman
climb a tree in the backyard,

into the high web-laden branches
and weep.

Place

This place, left of where you are.

Someone is there waving
who will not follow.

Her eyes are droopy blue
not smoky or significant.

The story here is about something
you would underline twice.
And the soft noises you make in your sleep.

Hinges joined with spaces in between.

Where I am desperate here on a
dock in the dark aquamarine.

Rosetta Ballew-Jennings

Household Haunting

In infancy, I found perpetual nervousness
and later, a woman in burgundy pants who calls out, "relief!" I say
to her, " Trickery, Trickery, Exhaustion"

The house is dancing on my head, is beckoning her objects, her
contents
to come back, to come out of my insides.

A narration of 7:00

The evening is close and outside
our children are eating chocolate Hostess cupcakes
and wrestling without using their arms.
A new game today.

One of my black and white movies is on
in the other room—the sounds gravelly and loose
and we are kissing and I was going to say
something about being gravelly and loose.
something about the coffee table.

The pieces have never really fit.

A kid is screaming haphazardly
and you go to check.

I throw a pork chop
at your right shoulder. You don't turn
just yip and kick
the chop to the dog waiting at the door.

The anecdote of people eating cantaloupe

Remove figure from the window
and watch it shutter away,
break away towards the sun, primarily stay the same,
and then,   not.

:We do it to say we did something: Like going to the bank.
Like eating cantaloupe. Like buying an expensive camera with
the option of black and white or color or vivid color.

:We do it for the movement: Thinking about how easy
it would be to rob the bank; noticing the placement of the cameras
in the lobby
and outside. Taking pictures of spiders on flowers. Taking
pictures of ourselves
nude in black and white and vivid color and in secret in the
bathrooms, or posed on step-ladders
and then sending them to _____. And then, eating
cantaloupe off of _____'s inside thigh
drawing patterns in/on the sweet sap.

:We do it because we don't know what else to do: Don't know
what else to do
and we do it. Just threaten to rob the bank. Anonymous phone
call. Take pictures
of green spiders on pink flowers up close, in vivid color, and send
them to our mother-in laws.
Take the other pictures and then call to have _____ delete
them, right away; apologize. Make
the date with cantaloupe, eat Chinese at a restaurant instead. Take
our tea to go.

And the window is the window and we look up
and the roof is gone. Maybe we will chase it.
Maybe we will open the doors.

Rosetta Ballew-Jennings

And.

I would leave. I would leave my potted plants. I would leave my
rose bush on the first step of my duplex with its roses pink and
yellow and as big as my hand. I would leave my husband. I would
leave my husband probably with the rose bush. I would leave my
photos of the people I do not know, though, I would like to keep
them and the photos of the people I do know. I would leave my
cat, but she is old and has very few teeth and I know that you
like cats, even old ones, so I have told her I would not have to
leave her, and I do not like to break promises. I would leave my
other promises. to me, to my lover, to the air. And I would leave
and we would find ourselves drinking coffee over newspapers.
drinking coffee over morning classic movies. drinking juice over
Anne Carson's essays. drinking orange juice over an itinerary to
a village in Italy that I told you I would like to see fully, being a
child and sick the last time I was there. drinking coffee and juice
over ourselves. And I would be uncomfortable. for now. forever.
for a moment. And I would be in love.

It is about the endurance, we think

You call me mystic. You bellow it down the hall.
The dog comes. It is kissed into my neck. The cat walks by.
Your call is repeated here. again and again.
We don't know what we are doing. We try it again in British accents,
clown noses. We vacuum. light candles. buy bread.

We call this "shared things," "misery," "Veronica." There should be
something else.

We go to the backyards, or maybe restaurants. We say hello. We get the mail.
We cut our hair. We wave.

Two halves of ground cared for by old girls and marbled children

1.

Yet they love wind

2.

They should go to where the season was still in full swing and
where new interests and new friends would distract
Isabel's mind from her unfortunate entanglement

3.

she could amuse herself in a dull moment
in a mall or airport by breaking down other women's gestures
and trying them out. Like square dancing: hundreds of calls.

4.

Fran and Emma sat down to rest. Fran's shoes were hurting her
feet. Emma's hat was falling in her eyes

5.

The new things
were tucked into a souvenir hat.

6.

Good bones. Great pieces.

7.
Today I am thinking about the truths of doll houses.

8.
Though, this time I made it about a woman with green beans
in a grocery store and not our imaginary affair.

9.
We are all saying the blue sky with one white cloud at a certain
point.

10.
One begins to wonder what adult voices sound like.

11.
Sometimes I think they are not really unlike children's voices,
just a little slower and more burdened

12.
I am picturing you saying it, slowly and as a burden.
It's calling: ATTEND. *Attend.*

13.
We didn't belong anywhere at all,
happy across the tall grass.

14.

The soft marble is weathered with the children's hair worn away, and the legs of the girl who is seated are missing. The name "Lars Schmidt" is barely visible.

The name of his sister is entirely worn away, but I have been told she was called Ruth.

The figures are about two feet tall.

15.

Yet they love the wind

The connecting of lines

In the connecting of lines, your shirt is half un-done
and I am across the room
at the kitchen counter,
two inches too low for vegetable chopping
and general stirring and the way you tried to press
yourself into me.

Pictures of outlines. Sometimes
there is just no stopping.

I have found you in the small bedroom
with a girl, legs barely long enough
to wrap around your rippled waist.
Her ripened cheeks turn
toward the twisting fan.

No template; no existing voice.

The smell of the fresh peach paint
only, and the sound of Canadian geese
end. front. middle.

Sounding to make sure
they are all there.

Rosetta Ballew-Jennings

That time you thought you had an understanding

I notice the ease of it.

The way a foot, either one really,
can sit in overlapped hands and
how I can push my knee up
against my lips.

It is human here,
and I don't think of anyone.

And, in the comfort of it,
three folds appear
in the skin around my hips,
which could last all evening.

Instead, the knock at the door, how I forgot
to vacuum. And taking the clean towel, the night before,
about how there was something else.

Something that I can't quite remember.

And then, still, something else.

There is no restoration of a youthful bohemian tale

There is something to say
about being lost
in the way something moves.

The swaying, shuffling, sailing
before sitting down again.
But you have never moved like that.

 I am never lost in you.

And the crickets on the concrete
are all wet and black.

All of this in a slick frame and
I don't recognize our faces.
I could step outside and take a picture.

But I know you are smiling and not moving.
I can't stay.

The glossy vines come down
wilted and wound in your hair.

There is not much I can do.

The man with the waved hair

The man's hands across the table
smooth and motioning, will not hold me.

He tells me the door. This door. This house.
I was there at lunch at noon. The bowed mailbox at nine.

He draws my name in the air. Draws it in houses,
stores, and streets. The places he is not.

The tulips are twisted and succumbing to the floor.
I am a forgettable woman
I am a forgettable woman with tulips

The stillness of the Chinese jar

In the end, the specifics evaporate and
there is no control here.

It is not the ordering of the stars, or
the hands and mouths
of children

It is
There is the mail. There is a size 12 footprint in
the middle of your back, somehow. There is brown sugar
sauce for carrots tonight.

9255 train, south

The train is stopped. It's always stopped.
The woman wants to go home
to her one toothed cat
and the death certificate on the wall—
her name except the middle name and completely unknown.
One woman died years before
the other was born. The train
is far away. And the later woman now
is talking to a sleeping man with earplugs.
To him, sound is quiet, a bastard boyfriend
speaking French. Bastard being a cliché
he prefers jumblegomph, same meaning
except the syllables haven't already had the experience—
something about mythology
and cat people and the way it will go on being cliché
until people aren't people
and everything is put in place and scheduled
like death. Maybe there never was a train. Expect, now,
the coffin-box is left open
to see the sky and the blue birds.

Savannah Boulevard at dawn

He says to her "Watch my hands. Just watch." And I don't
watch, moving two sidewalk squares with each step.

Instead, I imagine their names.

On the corner their hair is tangling
together in the dawn wind.

I know this man and this woman.
I have said their goodbyes.

On the banks of the canal

Everything here is still and bound up in water.
Motion without moving
causes that tree to be the same tree again
and again we are told, though we agree
the fruit has seemed to change
from apples to pears to apples to fruit.

Everything here is still and bound up and now
there are townspeople, or maybe,
just a few people
we pretend to know.

They are waving their hats and their colored scarves.
They are wishing us well on our journeys.
We are waving back, shouting the names we have given them.

What can I say in your house

besides hello? Can I swim in your pool?
Hey, I haven't seen you
in a while, the cats
greasy and mewing at our feet.

The cats greasy and mewing to the windows.

You tell me the story
of the circus train wreck. "Killed fifty" you say,
not knowing if it included the animals,
ochered, feathered, jeweled, and saddled.

Your finger is pointing above our heads
to the south where the flat stones
in the weed-eaten grass say
"The Fat Man." "Bearded Woman In Red."

They say "Baldy" and "Driver of 4"
and "Fire Jumper."

raised letters in brass.

Among them,
stone elephants are small and white,
small enough for children to ride.

And so the children ride,
making whooping sounds
and bucking their legs and raising up
in the stirrups,

performing for an Indiana cemetery,
scissoring and digging in the grass.

The thing that makes you follow the baseboards across the room

is not the thing that will bring you back.

Six, evening, and it is Sunday.
The music to you is light and unfamiliar

you say.

I know it well.

We speak of something yellow
and bright—how we saw it.
It means nothing.

You kiss me.

The chair, the tree, the table leg.
The soap has fallen from its dish.

Rosetta Ballew-Jennings

Waiting for the noon parade

The children in Lafayette square have grown old.
Their hair has curled and straightened, and then,
curled again with age. They have stopped playing, or maybe
we have just stopped watching them.

You told me you want to be one of those children, to wear a white cap,
walk hand-in-hand. I listen when I see you,
but responding is unnecessary beyond what to order, and the
address of where we are going next, as you know
I am terrible with north and like directions.
There is latency here or maybe,
a window with eight separate panes.
The way we hold each other's words in our mouths
and never let them gather with the air and wait, wondering
which way will the parade come

Miscellaneous locations

It takes concentration
to only feel the fingers on my face
in firm circles around the eyes, and the background noises.

And everything is in a line

mussed and jumbled, but still in a line.
or something we could call a line, or pretend.
The rainbows of suds, a few, glinting about.

The randomness of it

all. You know, you won't find anything here
or in the way we arrive.

It is how lipstick clings to crystal glasses
without any pattern
and how I never raise my hand to say goodbye.

It is how there was something you were going to say,

something about the way I am.

Tell me something

After the blown trees, we pass ourselves
several times, and from several angles,
so that it's not even us anymore,
or pretend, or the park again. Stars and stars.

Then, we can just say, "walk in the park," or "star gazing"
to those who pass by
and not mention the crooked bricks underfoot
or the boats.

Everyone is looking. Have you noticed.

There is the loud comfort of noises around
and the green sage just in case. Or the illusion of it.

But that is only for me, as such things, you say,
are such things passing.

And, you know, our clothes will never be put away.

I think this is the story of a gesture
and the way things are lost.
And how much brighter that streetlight is
than that one.

The construction site

For Martha

1.

The red plastic tulips from friends in 1972.

2.

Visitors in the parlor, Visitors in the other rooms.

3.

Friend in the pink chair. The body in the brown chair.

4.

The window undone:

5.

the shoulders undone.

6.

With red curved tile:

7.

twelve men build
a third floor of ten rooms.

As if she were something opened

> True desire is when your whole being is soaked in the
> image of your desire and you cannot see the difference
> between your desire and the physical world around you.
> —*Tulshi Sen*

As if she were something opened,
exposed to immeasurable space
she lines the walls with herself—

desire between the window panes and flush
against the outlet-plate screws.

I know from her, it is a haphazard embodiment—
She doesn't know how to be the room.

And then,
she is the house.

I love her. She is the house. I am among others.
She is the house. It matters only as much
as it matters. She is the house.
She is the house opened up to the sky.
True desire.

And the people? Perpetually stationed
at the mailbox and signposts

waiting for rain, or maybe a tornado
and we are taking bets on what comes first and
who will last.

Cemetery

For Kathleen

But Lucy
your eyes.

            – Jean Valentine
          from "Your Picture"

1.

Because I could no longer be with the house
I go to

look for the babies
Sometimes this is enough

In absence of arms and cloth

Sometimes I find purple
clematis   weathered peonies in dark pink

2.

The bones of your lips

are not the bones of your
eyes or the spine

But
the bones of the fingers are best

The frame of the body collected

The frame of the body dismantled

Three bones   Three junctions

And all the different names and
places you make with them

3.

Sam is a dog in the yard
thirteen dogs

with the same name

The girl puts her dandelions there
under the metal sign

I've heard you keep her drawings
in the gun safe

The letters too

Can you breathe all night?

She'll hear that you killed a man
Or more

later

She'll keep the aluminum cans

She'll keep your wife's clothespin bag and live
in various houses

4.

The people are in the fields and
Some of the waters too

The woman has gone to see them

nothing more

5.

The people are in the fields and
some of the waters

and then they are under

The others are waiting for word
the colors of this new sky   the patterns
of the stars   the textures of grasses

6.

Baby Girl Reasoner is my favorite

By herself

Under the peonies
She does not exist in paper

My mother exists in paper
but not in water   and tells me on various stoops
she doesn't want of stone
either

I tell her

peonies

magenta roses

that she will not be tricked with metal

7.

A body in the hill
A body in the fire

Two husbands
A wife with an infant child

Different hills.   fires.

I am just saying
the same eyes should be all together

Rosetta Ballew-Jennings

8.

For the Infant Boy: November 12, 1958,

Even the watercress and the crepe
myrtles that come up between
your toes

have two names

9.

How many days were there picnics at these shut-ins?

Chicken   tomatoes   gooseberries

The singing and wading The rock-to-rock games
The sliding through these shut-ins

And how many children in general were here
And then
    how many were carried down and away

                        And how many   And the
dogs

                        Numbered
                        The tibulas   The perch   The
igneous rock

10.

The hill with my husband's last name
will take me without a box

or
with a simple box

and beetles

There are peonies at the fenced corners
A man named Ambrose to the east

Delpha to the west

I must have the beetles
Please do not forget

I am afraid of fire

Please do not forget
what I am afraid of

11.

What bone caressed my brother's ankle
coddled his ribs as he fell
in the ocean-opened grave?

I imagine him in purple silk
A white-steepled
church, Bones

The colors have seeped into the tree roots

Dirt that smells like ground
Ground that smells like leaves and walnuts

Bones

Bones, there are ships in the trees
Have you heard?

12.

Do the angels and the concreted children
ever wonder about the absence

of fruit and muslin here

13.

A woman. a tree.
the woman as an ornament. the tree.
swaying. the dropped mulberries. few by few.
wave petunias. sound
red geraniums. us reading. her stomach.

 : "A song from your banjo, please"

Rosetta Ballew-Jennings

14.

Claudia, who would haunt him
loves pines
portrait broaches   egg and dart molding

The three in her house now
couldn't know this

15.

The frame of the body collected

The frame of the body dismantled

Have you pulled
apart the lips and
looked for the face

underneath

The basis/basics

16.

For Corey

Two young men and their heads
are open

Their eyes in the brains
in the bricks

But their teeth:

constellations

diamond-like under a flashlight

17.

The bones of your lips

are not the bones of your
eyes or the spine

But
the bones of the fingers are best

Apart
We can hang them from the cedars

Or thread them—
Eggshell colored rings on the bayberry branches

Rosetta Ballew-Jennings

18.

How will they want your flowers
your hands

Few understand hair wreaths
hold depths
spoken passably

real lockets too
And

the photos of dead children
colored by hand in kitchens
hiding in bureau drawers

We must not leave them behind   Remind me

I had six shades of peonies from twelve bushes
that I wanted to send to you

full bloom
but the ants ————

19.

Without the squirrels
Ruth and Lars are lonely

The others forgot to leave them
bikes
or blankets

So we put the peanuts on
their shoes   tuck them toward
the legs

Name the squirrels
The ones that chatter

Decorate Ruth's hair with daisies
Lars' hands are filled with light pink
peonies

We go home
and put things on shelves
Paint small pictures of our mothers and cats

Rosetta Ballew-Jennings

20.

The woman is in the houses
The woman is in the fields and some of the waters

And then she is
the ocean and a eucalyptus tree left with a friend

For your other name

Who is this stranger in a dead president's house
holding her hand to the quilted bedspread
that she isn't supposed to touch

that takes your thinking, by accident of course,
down the wallpaper and across the cherry-painted floor?

For this living woman there is no elegy here
that you sign your name across

and read in your own voice, but hear hers
as it comes back

off of yourself, reading there,

these poorly done walls in Kansas
and Atlanta. In Savannah,

all the various places you've been.

Here is her face at your neck.
And this time, unlike other times

you touch her and she touches back.

Touches you and you feel it
in your other name.

Guided mountain tour

She is five and naming the running

proghorn antelopes. Mox, Teeny, Cat, Baby,

Spot, Boo   I couldn't tell you why

The fleet panicked:

Boo and Baby broke the wrong way. Quick.

Kicked and tumbled over the east cataract

                                        Together

their's   her's   all at once

epistemic eyes

Coda

A confusion   upheaval

A turn outward,

     inward

Silence.

And then,

evening—

the uneven beats
of locusts and one owl

NOTES

Epigraph:	Excerpt of "Autumn Day" from *The Door in the Mountain* by Jean Valentine
44-46	Some poem sections draw upon extended email conversations and books: *The Razor's Edge, Crossing a Memoir, Graveyards of Chicago,* and *Fancy Dance in Chicken Town.*
55-56	Poem contains names on headstones from the Showmen's Rest area of the Woodlawn Cemetery in Forest Park, Illinois. The Showmen's Rest Area of the cemetery began with the burial – human and animal – of the Hagenbeck-Wallace circus train wreck and fire on June 22, 1918. Many of the performers and circus hands were unidentifiable or their real identities unknown, thus many of the headstones display descriptions, nicknames, or the circus position performed by the deceased.
63	Excerpt of "Your Picture" from *Lucy* by Jean Valentine
76	"Claudia, who would haunt him" is a chapter title from John Irving's *Until I Find You.*

ABOUT THE POET

Rosetta J. Ballew-Jennings is most at ease amidst the moxie of old houses and cemeteries. She is fond of home concoctions and remedies, half-begun projects, and made-for-television movies. Her MFA is from Texas State University, and she currently lives in historic Saint Joseph, Missouri. This is her debut poetry collection.

www.ingramcontent.com/pod-product-compliance
Lightning Source LLC
Chambersburg PA
CBHW020214090426

42734CB00008B/1064